# GRANDMA HEKMATT REMEMBERS

Text © 2003 by Ann Morris

Photographs and illustrations © 2003 by Peter Linenthal

Other photographs courtesy of Hekmatt Khattab

Thanks to Stephen Brown for his help.


Library of Congress Cataloging-in-Publication Data


Morris, Ann, 1930-

Grandma Hekmatt remembers: an Arab-American family story/Ann

Morris; photographs and illustrations by Peter Linenthal.

p. cm.—(What was it like, grandma?)

Summary: Three Arab-American girls learn about their family and

cultural history from their grandmother, who grew up in Cairo, Egypt,

and moved to New Jersey after her marriage. Includes directions for

making Egyptian paper boats.

ISBN 0-7613-2864-5 (lib. ed.) — ISBN 0-7613-1944-1 (pbk.)

1. Egypt—Juvenile literature.   [1. Arab Americans—New Jersey.

2. Egypt. 3. Grandmothers.]   I. Linenthal, Peter, ill.   II. Title.


DT49.M66 2003        305.892'7620749—dc21        2003000693


The Millbrook Press, Inc.

2 Old New Milford Road

Brookfield, Connecticut 06804

www.millbrookpress.com

What Was It Like, Grandma?

# GRANDMA HEKMATT REMEMBERS

## An Arab-American Family Story

**Ann Morris**
**Photographs and illustrations by Peter Linenthal**

**The Millbrook Press**
**Brookfield, Connecticut**

**Hekmatt and Hedaiet's house in Wayne, New Jersey**

# Suzanne, Yasmine, and Sarah are Arab-American girls.

They live with their parents Amanny, a teacher, and Hossan, a doctor, in Wayne, New Jersey.

Their grandmother Hekmatt and grandfather Hedaiet live nearby in a two-story white house. The children call their grandmother Setto and their grandfather Getto, the Arabic words for grandma and grandpa.

Suzanne, age seven, Yasmine, age five and a half, and
Sarah, age four, with their grandparents Hedaiet and Hekmatt

It's a good thing that the children live so close to their grandparents, because they really enjoy spending time with them. And their grandparents enjoy spending time with them.

The children do many wonderful things when they get together with Grandma Hekmatt and Grandpa Hedaiet. In their grandparents' backyard the children play on the swings, and they roll around in the green grass.

In their grandparent's living room the children sometimes belly dance.

Belly dancing is a favorite kind of dancing in Egypt, the country where Hekmatt and Hedaiet came from.

**Sometimes Grandma Hekmatt reads to the girls when they visit.**

She and Grandpa Hedaiet teach them Arabic words and show them how to write in the Arabic alphabet.

Before she leaves her grandparents' home, Sarah helps Grandma Hekmatt straighten up the house.

# Grandma Hekmatt and Grandpa Hedaiet grew up in Cairo, the capital of Egypt.

Hekmatt says that Egypt is the center of the Middle East. Many tourists come to see the pyramids. The Egyptian people are very warm and friendly. They have good schools and universities and lots of farms.

Hekmatt and Hedaiet didn't meet until they were in college. Hekmatt went to college in Egypt, and Hedaiet studied in the United States. But once when Hedaiet returned to Egypt for a visit, he met Hekmatt and they soon married. Then Hekmatt came back to the United States with Hedaiet, and there they had their two children, Amanny and Tamer.

At first Hekmatt didn't like the United States. She missed her family, and she didn't know how to speak English very well. But gradually she learned the language and got used to the many things that made her life easier here, such as cars. In Egypt, Hekmatt walked everywhere.

**Cairo is a bustling city on the Nile River.**

Grandma Hekmatt has many memories of growing up in Egypt. She remembers playing with her brother and sisters and visiting her grandfather, who had a big farm not far from Cairo. She remembers visiting the Great Pyramids at Giza, another city on the Nile, and going to the beach at Alexandria, about 100 miles (160 kilometers) away. Most of all she remembers her home.

"When I was a child," she tells her grandchildren, "we didn't get a refrigerator until I was ten years old. But the food was very fresh. Each day a man came and brought bread, cheese, fresh vegetables, and fresh meat.

# We didn't have a TV either."

Sometimes Hekmatt shows the children an album of family photos. She tells them about her family and life in Egypt.

**Here is Hekmatt as a baby in Egypt with her mother, father, brother, and two sisters.**

Here is Hekmatt (far right) posing for a picture with her college classmates on the steps of one of Egypt's Great Pyramids.

Here is Hekmatt as a young mother holding her daughter Amanny, the children's mother.

Although Hekmatt and Hedaiet live thousands of miles away from their families, they often return to Egypt to visit. When Amanny was a girl, they used to take her along with them.

**On a trip to Egypt, Grandpa Hedaiet and Amanny pose before the Great Pyramids at Giza.**

# Grandma Hekmatt's house is filled with many things that she has brought back from Egypt.

She enjoys telling her granddaughters about each of them. She shows the children a blue clay *hamsa* that usually hangs on the wall in the living room. Hekmatt explains that a hamsa is supposed to keep bad things away and is a symbol for good luck.

Amanny shows the children an Egyptian water jar. "These are water jars to keep you from getting thirsty in the desert," she says.

# Sometimes on a rainy afternoon, the children make crafts or play games.

Today, their grandmother shows them how to make Egyptian boats out of paper that they can sail in a tub. Hekmatt explains that when she was a girl she used to make these same little boats with her mother and sail them in her bathtub.

# Egyptian Paper Boats

To make Egyptian paper boats, all you need is an 8½ x 11 inch piece of paper.

HERE IS WHAT YOU DO:

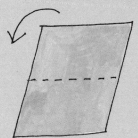

Fold 8½ x 11"
sheet of paper
in half,

like this.

Then fold and unfold in the
opposite direction to make
a crease down the center.

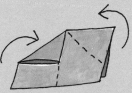

Fold top corners
in to center
crease

like this.

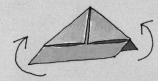

Fold flaps at bottom
up to the front and
up to the back

like this.

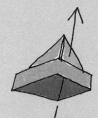

Hold at center of
front and back
and move apart,

and tuck one flap
behind the other
like this.

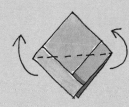

Fold bottom up at
the front, and up
at the back.

Then turn the little
triangle to the side
like this,

and pull sides out while
pushing up with
thumbs.

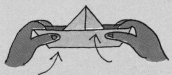

Move thumbs and guide
sides up, and there's

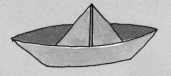

your boat!

Grandma Hekmatt enjoys cooking. Sometimes after school she lets the children help her bake delicious cookies called *kahek*.

## The children have become expert bakers. And expert eaters, too!

First they make
the cookie dough
and filling.

Then they shape the
cookies and put them
on cookie sheets.

After the cookies are baked, the
children sprinkle powdered sugar
on them.

Now the cookies are ready to eat.

**The family worships at a mosque near Hekmatt's home.**

# Like many Arab Americans, Grandma Hekmatt and her family are Muslims, followers of the religion of Islam.

In the Islamic tradition, Amanny puts the *hejab*, a head covering, on the children at the mosque. The hejab is worn for modesty. Many Arab women wear the hejab in and outside the home. The girls pray together with their grandmother.

# In this mosque the women sit upstairs and the men sit downstairs.

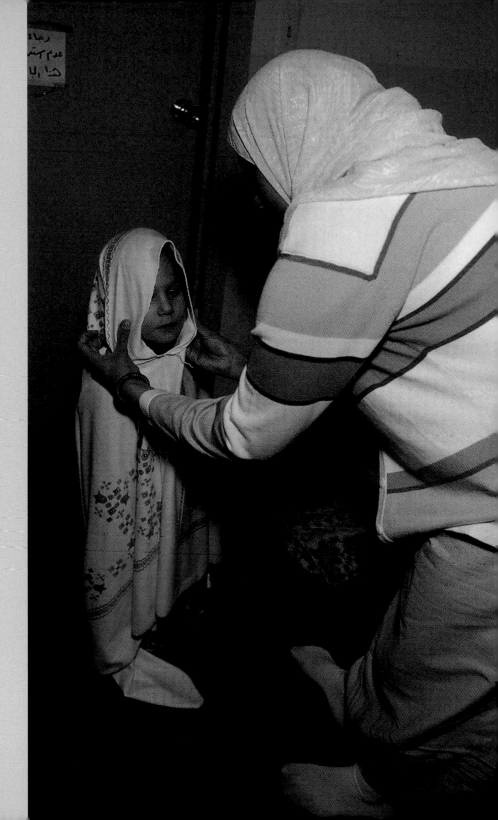

After the service, the family returns to their grandparents' house.

## Hekmatt shows the children a clock in the shape of the mosque.

It has special buttons to push that sound the call to prayer.

# Ramadan is a special
# holy month for Muslims.

At the end of Ramadan Muslims celebrate with
special feasts. They visit with family and friends.

# Grandma Hekmatt has two beautiful golden lamps called fanous that were made for the festival of Ramadan.

Amanny explains that in Egypt during Ramadan, children put candles in these lamps and wave them as they go up and down the streets at the end of each day. People along the way give the children candies and other treats.

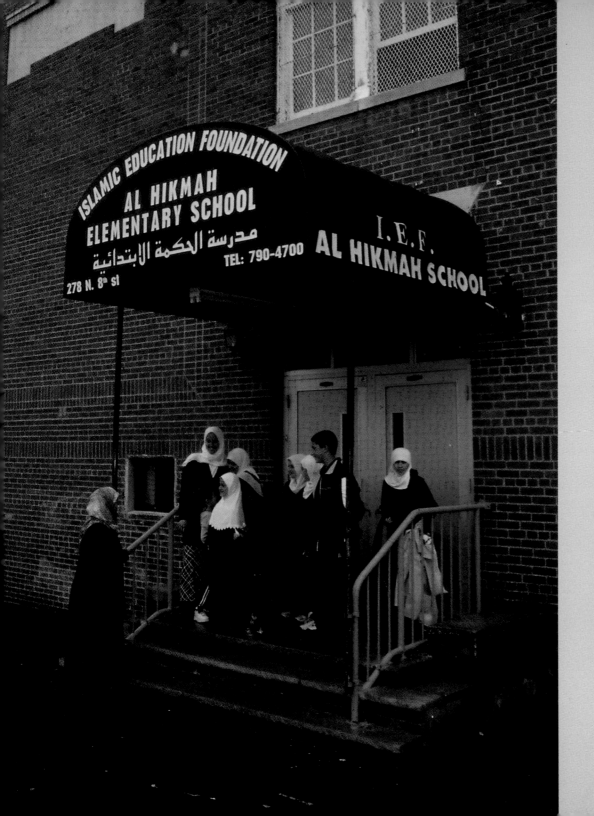

Not too far from their house is the Muslim school where Suzanne, Yasmine, and Sarah go each day. Amanny is a teacher there, so it is easy for her to drop by to see what they are learning.

Sometimes Grandma Hekmatt comes to see what they are doing in school, too. The children show her what they are studying and how they can use the computer.

The children
are proud to
be able to
read and write
both in English
and in Arabic.

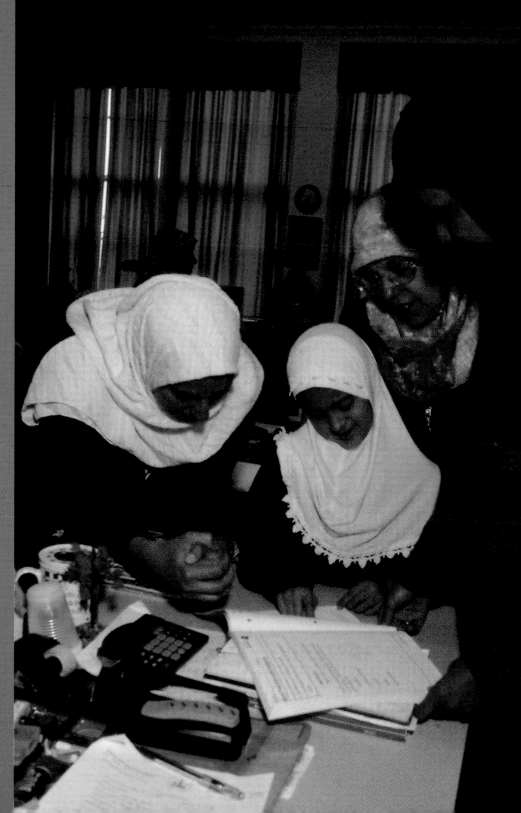

The school picnic is a place for fun and games. The whole family comes to join the children, their classmates, and their teachers at the picnic—including their mom and dad and their grandparents.

**Everybody has a good time eating, playing games, and talking.**

While the family thinks that Egypt is a great country, they also believe that the United States is the best place in the world to live!

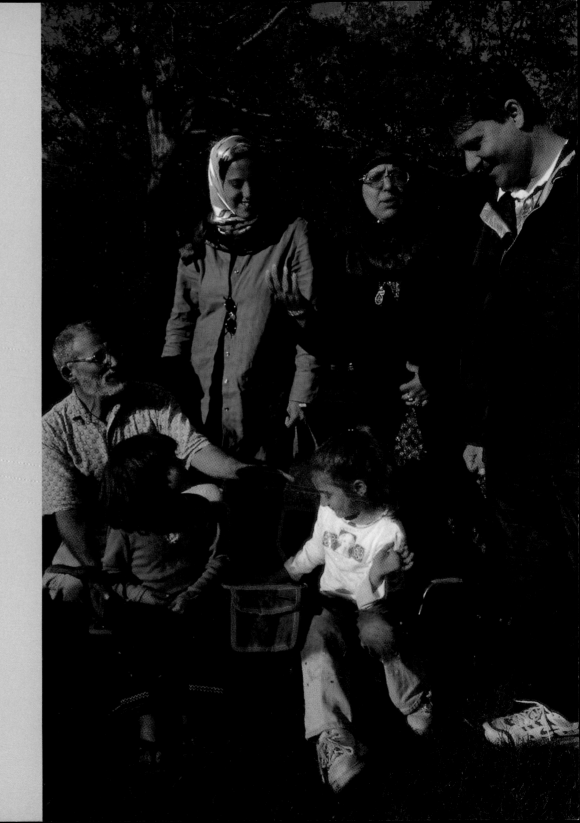

# ALL ABOUT MY FAMILY

## Would you like to know more about your family? Here are some things you can do.

### INTERVIEWS

You will find out many interesting things about your relatives by interviewing them. Ask them questions about their childhood—where they lived, what they liked best to do and to eat, what they read and studied in school. Find out, too, how things are different today from when they were young. Use a tape recorder to record your questions and their answers.

### FAMILY ALBUM

Ask your relatives for pictures of themselves. Put all the pictures in an album. Write something you have learned about each person under his or her picture.

### FAMILY TREE

All of us have many relatives. Some of us are born into the family. Others are related by marriage or have been adopted. You can make a family tree to show who belongs to your family.

# SPECIAL WORDS

**Hamsa:** A traditional charm in the shape of a hand used for good luck

**Hejab:** A long scarf used by Muslim women to cover their heads

**Islam:** The religion of Muslims

**Koran:** A book of sacred writing read by Muslims

**Mosque:** The place where Muslims go to pray and worship

**Muslims:** People who believe in the religion of Islam

**Ramadan:** A special holy month of worship for Muslims that ends with three days of feasts with family and friends

# KHATTAB FAMILY TREE

Hekmatt

Hedaiet

Amanny

Tamer

Hossan

Suzanne

Yasmine

Sarah